William Benbow

GRAND NATIONAL HOLIDAY AND CONGRESS OF THE PRODUCTIVE CLASSES

* * * * * * *

SELECTION OF EROTICA FROM THE RAMBLER'S MAGAZINE

* * * * * * *

Edited and Introduced by S.A. Bushell

PELAGIAN PRESS
BCM Signpost
London
WC1N 3XX

Announcement to all Employers, and the Self-Employed from The Royal Commission on the Quality of Life.

Government health advisors, as well as the most respected commentators on social well-being, have informed us that the benefits accrued by the intensification of work are now being outweighed by severe hidden costs. These include crime, stress-related illnesses, feelings of powerlessness, despair and a marked reluctance on the part of citizens to engage in community activities. All told, according to the most sophisticated cost-benefit analysis methods, the net loss achieved by the 'work revolution' to the country has been estimated at £100 billion.

In the light of these disturbing findings, it has been decided that drastic cost-cutting measures are necessary. From August 12, 1995 it has been decreed that all traditional festivals, feasts, wakes and holidays of any religion practised within the United Kingdom shall be observed by all citizens, regardless of race or religion. Furthermore, in order to facilitate an immediate reduction in the rate of work performed by the community Monday is hereby designated a Holiday indefinitely. Only emergency work may be performed on holidays and must be paid at triple-time rate. Street-parties, feasts and communal celebrations are to be encouraged in all regions. Any employer found promoting non-essential labour shall be subject to fines of not less that £50,000 for each offence. Furthermore all essential non-paid labour is to be performed by anyone other than the person usually designated to carry it out. It has been estimated that the expected reduction in the burden of house-work upon its usual agents will lead to a saving in the NHS tranquilliser budget of 20%.

We acknowledge that employers may find these regulations onerous, not to say threatening to their continuing survival. However the Commission has found that 80-90% of all work performed in the United Kingdom to be of a highly specious nature, and that its benefit to the nation seems to be little more than keeping people off the streets. In the event that you may be one of the employers liquidated, could we refer you to the excellent booklet 'How to live in a World without Work' published by the Saint Monday Observance Society. In the light of the today's global economy we are working with our partners in the EC to introduce the concept of the Grand International Holiday in order to ensure fair competition between all trading nations.

In conclusion we would like to emphasise that the above regulations provide us with a unique opportunity to press ahead with the government's goals of maximising conviviality, increasing the happiness of all the community and ensuring that individuals have the freedom to idle, chat, relax and party.

Introduction

Anyone delving into the history of resistance and revolt in Britain will eventually come across the shadowy figure of William Benbow. Whether the initial enquiry is into the 1926 General Strike, or the Chartists, or organised blasphemy, William Benbow crops up as an influence, an organiser or an inspiration. One of the first histories of the 1926 General Strike [1] opens with a chapter on Benbow. The Chartists initiated some of their most dramatic and ambitious actions inspired by his ideas. 19th century blasphemers, atheists and pornographers found in Benbow a champion and a promoter. Yet little is known of this mercurial Mancunian. In the 1830s he can be found rousing a crowd at The Rotunda in the pages of the **Poor Man's Guardian.** He can be found in the court reports of the King Bench (charged with anything from obscene libel to sedition). He can be found as a forlorn member of a long list of Chartist prisoners in the 1840 **Northern Star**, but discovering him is not to know him. There are few accounts of Benbow, unless they are insults or legal charges. He belongs in the ranks of the unknown subversives, i.e.those who do the dirty work and don't care who gets the credit.

From the 1790s to well into the 1840s the State in the British Isles faced perhaps one of the most sustained assaults on its order. Focused in the main on the issue of parliamentary reform, the ideals and practice of many of the men and women involved went beyond the demand to extend the franchise. The cry of "Parliamentary Reform" could be heard from many quarters, but while for some, such as Henry Brougham, it was a necessary measure of improvement the better to secure the status quo, for others such as the Tyneside agrarian radical, Thomas Spence, it was to be a prelude for the overthrow of tyranny and oppression, a time when there would 'neither Lords nor Landlords'.[2]

The challenge to tyranny and oppression came from many fronts. At the beginning of the 19th century the Luddites shook the new factory-owners and their supporters. Later the march of the Manchester Blanketeers (1817) and the rising in Derby (of the same year) served to keep the ruling classes in a state of high anxiety. While the 1820s saw something of a lull in mass actions, by the end of the decade the game of subversion was once more afoot as movements recovered from the period of repression following the crushing of the Cato Street Conspiracy (1820). Agitators in the cities once more gathered together masses of people in favour of extending the franchise (the ultras wanted universal manhood suffrage at least,others vacillated in response to political events). Labourers in the countryside were asserting their own particular right to existence by engaging in an extensive campaign of threatening letters and rick burnings led by the ubiquitous and probably non-existent Captain Swing. When the so-called Great Reform Act of 1832 was passed it proved to be a massive disappointment for those who had done most, and suffered most, to bring it into being. Working class agitation had led to middle class enfranchisement, so the nascent organisations of independent working class activity, such as the National Union of the Working Classes (NUWC) intensified their prominence and their activity. In the coming struggles, against the punitive Poor Law Amendment Act (1834) and for improvements in factory conditions, the NUWC was to self-destruct and the London Working Men's Association was to appear, and from these movements the idea of The Charter was conceived, a 6 point plan for the emancipation of the people of the British Isles(1838).

William Benbow's life straddled these events. He was 32 when he was sent by the Manchester radicals to stir up the country prior to the Blanketeer Marches, he was 36 when his printing and publishing business so captured the ribald and rebellious popular mood over the Queen Caroline affair[3] that he ended up in jail in 1821 for his caricatures of George IV, and 48 when he published his startling pamphlet Grand National Holiday and Congress of the Productive Classes for the NUWC in 1832. 1840 found him back in jail following the abortive attempt of the Chartists to institute his Holiday . The last sight we have of him is as a 68 year old addressing the Finsbury Manhood Suffrage Society in October 1852. Neither the date nor the circumstances of his death are known.

Benbow belonged to the underworld of radical activity, rather than to the pantheon of famous names - Hunt, Cobbett, Burdett. He seems to have been taken by the revolutionary ideas of Thomas Spence rather than the utilitarian notions of the leader of the respectable faction of working class radicalism, Francis Place. Indeed of all the physical force radicals of the time, he seems to be the most consistent and the most formidable. Ostensible 'physical forcers' like Feargus O'Connor gave him a wide berth. One of the first records of Benbow's speeches includes the defence of the right every man to bear arms (Manchester 1817). However the distinction between physical forcers and moral forcers should not be exaggerated. Benbow was a small business man (printer, coffee shop owner, fruiterer) as well as an artisan (shoemaker) and he did much to build up the institutions of the radical movement, including setting up the Theobalds Road Institute (in which his second wife ran The Female Society) and being a leading light in the British Association for the Promotion of Co-Operative Knowledge.

Benbow challenged the corrupt and draconian order of emergent 19th century capitalism in two ways. On the one hand a fighter against *exclusion*, exclusion of the people from political power and cultural experience, on the other a propagator of *secession*, secession from a State which operated in the interest of only a minority. The apparently contradictory nature of holding these two views can perhaps be resolved by saying that the latter was a tactic to achieve the former. However, the vehemence of his rhetoric in Grand National Holiday, and his promotion of marginal, underground, culture might indicate that his real inclination was for a revolutionary break with the ruling institutions.

Benbow ran and supported what were called 'free-and-easies'(convivial gatherings of radicals in taverns),infidel chapels (blasphemous ceremonies of atheism or deism) as well as his coffee shop. Parliament was not the only thing he tried to subvert. In 1819 he was the chief advocate of a plan (thought up by Cobbett) to flood the country with forged bank notes in order to bring down the currency. In 1822 he was prosecuted by the Society for the Suppression of Vice for publishing pornography. And through all this he remained a Christian .

The publication of the Grand National Holiday pamphlet can be seen as the clarification of those tendencies in the radical movement which questioned the right of the British State to rule at all, including the Parliament which they worked so hard to reform. This is much more than the first call for a General Strike (a cessation of labour by all the people), it was an explicitly revolutionary proposal for an alternative convention, a General Congress which would circumvent the corrupt institutions of the British State. These institutions had failed. Even their reform had not brought justice. Benbow articulated, in the same spirit as anarchism, a profound suspicion of the state, and a need for the people to create institutions of their own.

The NUWC were only persuaded to publish the pamphlet when the House of Lords threw out the Reform Bill at the beginning of 1832. This was the beginning of a disillusionment confirmed not only by the deliberate exclusion of the working classes from the franchise, but by severity of the laws passed by the reformed Commons. The Poor Law Amendment Act, the Anatomy Acts,the General Enclosure Act and the failure of the Commons to restrict the working day to 10 hours gave the more radical views of Benbow greater appeal. Events had conspired to make the ideas put forward in Grand National Holiday particularly pertinent.

In this short pamphlet Benbow argued for a month long cessation of work, the provisioning of the people through an expropriation of the expropriators and the setting up of an alternative parliament based on universal suffrage which would decide on how to rid the country of the misery which had been inflicted upon it. This General Strike would, at the same time, take the form of a *holiday*, a holiday designed to increase the ease, gaiety,pleasure and happiness of the majority - a real 'festival of the oppressed'

The ideas themselves were not new, although the manner of their presentation was. As Benbow takes pains to point out, the 'political holiday' where hierarchical relations are dissolved can be found in the Bible (Leviticus 25)[4]. The first to use the biblical Jubilee as a metaphor for revolt was Thomas Spence ('the unfee'd advocate of the disinherited seed of Adam'as he described himself,see note 2) in his 1782 Jubilee Hymn[5]. Today's notion of a Jubilee - as a celebration of kings and popes - already existed, of course. Although the idea of the Jubilee was used during the English Civil War it was as an example of a crucial balancing mechanism in an agrarian society[6] rather than as a model for the overthrow of power. Perhaps it needed the dissolution of that agrarian society for the idea to gain a revolutionary meaning. Certainly by the time Benbow was writing many radicals had used the notion to express their vision of revolutionary change. The radical Jacobin, Maurice Margarot, on return from his spell of transportation following London Corresponding Society political activity in the 1790s, wrote his last will and testament: **Proposal for a Grand National Jubilee: Restoring to Every Man his Own and thereby extinguishing both Want and War** (1810)[7].In this he argued for every person in England to have five acres of land, and went on to conspire with the revolutionary French to invade Britain and restore the Saxon constitution. This notion of the lost constitution, although sensibly not given any prominence in Benbow's pamphlet, draws on a supposition which was always present in the radical movement, and which Benbow's pamphlet reinforced. This was the idea of the utter illegitimacy of the current ruling institutions, the idea that the State is simply a usurpation of powers,that it was beyond reform.

Benbow's proposal for a Congress of the Productive Classes echoes a concern first aired by the Levellers in the English Civil War. The argument went that the governing institutions of the British state cannot be trusted, that a rival convention should be set up by the people acting for themselves. For Benbow the people are defined as those outside the governmental and institutional system (this included the municipal apparatus) and who are to be encouraged to disobey it.

> *Government is a distinct body, and that it has no feeling for, nor interests in common with the* ***people*** *!...The Government, the Clergy, the Squirearchy, and the non-producers, are a distinct body from the people. The Government is a complicated system of tyranny, of the worst class.* William Benbow **Agitator** Nov.1833

The solution to the irreformability of the British State was to turn your back on it and the agent of this change must be the working classes themselves:

To expect aid from Tories, Whigs, Liberals - to expect aid from the middling classes, or from any other class than those who suffer, (from the working classes), is sheer madness! (GNH)

The idea of independent working class activity is not unequivocally promoted by Benbow in this pamphlet. The pamphlet is itself addressed to the 'Productive Classes', an old radical phrase distinguishing the people from the parasitocracy of the State, Church, sinecurists and money-lenders. It included farmers, factory-owners , even shop-keepers. But this delineation was beginning to become suspect. The middle classes had proved to be far more concerned about their own interests than of those of the population as a whole. The radical papers of the day continually harped on about the betrayal they felt from the 'shopocracy', but right into the 1840s the idea that there was no fundamental division of interest between the labourers and their employers existed amongst radical leaders, even while labourers, rural and urban, experienced the opposite. Similarly, radical strategy on the whole stuck to the idea that the root of popular misery was exclusion from political power, rather than the social and economic system itself. When the State began to implement ameliorative measures in the 1840s this radical ideology was undermined.

Benbow reveals these confusions more clearly than most. Had his plan for the Holiday taken place, the expropriations he envisaged would have called more than parliamentary structures into question. Similarly his support of the ranting, millenarian, dangerous underworld of the London 'free-and-easies' does not easily fit into the respectable populist image of a reformer seeking merely to include in the fruits of civilisation those who had been unjustly ostracised. Like most of us, he was right in some things and wrong in others. The fact that emergent capitalism required the services of the 'Old Corruption' in order to consolidate itself and expand should warn us about the dangers of making too clean a break between the 'social and economic' and the 'political'[8]. Without the introduction of paper money, without parliamentary enclosure, without state repression of the Luddites and Blanketeers capitalism would have found the going considerably heavier. While the root of the evil for Benbow clearly was the despotic system of government, his remedies and practice took him beyond reform to the edge of revolution. The fact that he emphasised the political rather than social[9] origins of mass misery in the 19th century points to one of the reasons for Chartism's failure but it doesn't neutralise the revolutionary implications of the project he initiated.

Grand National Holiday sold well and soon needed another reprint. On its publication the NUWC called for simultaneous meetings throughout the country, and although the London one was banned meetings held in both Manchester and Huddersfield endorsed the plan for a National Convention. The idea of the 'holiday' became a constantly discussed tactic within the radical movement, it once more being endorsed in 1834 by the London committee set up to defend the Dorchester trades unionists (The Tolpuddle Martyrs). However the NUWC was by no means united behind Benbow's tactics. William Lovett for one, believed Benbow's violent rhetoric to have put people off joining the organisation and was eventually to blame him for its demise. Throughout the 1830s no systematic attempt was made to implement the plan, although it remained a constant subject of discussion amongst radicals.

It seems fair to speculate that part of the popularity of the idea lay in its call for a holiday. Official holidays had been whittled down to 4 in a year from the 17 enjoyed the previous century. At the same time there were enough survivals of the old feasts and pastimes to remind people that a life of work had not been the perpetual experience of the people. The radical paper **Poor Man's Guardian** was alert to the assault on the customs and feasts of the poor, and imposing industrial discipline on people with memories of week long wakes and Whitsun saturnalias was a problem frequently mentioned by industrialists. A Holiday could only be attractive for the working many who routinely toiled for 12 hours a day 6 days a week and it was an idea fruitfully used by radicals to counter-act the rituals and ceremonies of state.

When William IV expressed anxiety about the deaths from an outbreak of cholera in 1832, his government organised a Fast, whereby the middling and upper order could vent their guilt in a day's abstinence. The response of the radical movement was sharp:

> ***Freedom's Feast and Folly's Fast - March 21st***
>
> *Arrangements will be made to set an example to the industrious and useful classes of the nation, by the men of Mary-le-bone, to hold a grand holiday to liberty of mind and unity of action, on the above day at 36, Castle St., east of Oxford Market, to show the useless and idle classes of society that we will no longer cringe to hypocrisy and deception.* Poor Man's Guardian Feb.18 1832

In the demonstration of 100,000 that followed William Benbow and others were arrested as the authorities strove to prevent the crowd from parading throughout London. The Feast went ahead however, with parties of 50 or a 100 demonstrators partaking of a good dinner.

But it was near the end of the 1830s that the Holiday came closest to being realised. Benbow had been touring the North on a horse and cart spreading the idea and selling copies of his pamphlet. Mass agitations against the Poor Law

Amendment Act of 1834 had yielded nothing and the NUWC had collapsed. However out of these experiences new organisations emerged to form The Charter. A Petition was organised and presented to Parliament on July 12th 1839. Its prompt dismissal by the Commons threw the movement into a debate about what to do next and the idea of a 'National Holiday' re-appeared. By 13 votes to 6 the Chartist Convention agreed to support it.The Holiday was to begin on August 12th and the new Trades Unions were encouraged to help in its organisation.

There are many reasons for the failure of the Chartists to take the Holiday. In the first place the Chartists were themselves split over tactics, with some regarding the Holiday as tantamount to armed insurrection (a view Benbow did little to dispel) which they could not support on moral grounds. However even those who supported the Holiday regarded the announcement of the August 12 kick-off as hopelessly inept. Little preparation of the people had taken place both in terms of ideas and provisions. The state of trade in the country was poor enough for strike action to be ridden out by the employers, nor had anyone considered the military balance of forces. As the Leeds-based **Northern Star** put it in its August editorial : "ANY ATTEMPT TO BRING ABOUT THE SACRED MONTH BEFORE AN UNIVERSAL ARMING SHALL HAVE TAKEN PLACE,WILL RUIN ALL." Given Benbow's predilection for arming the people one would have thought he might have warned on this as well. But Benbow had himself been arrested on August 4th in Stockport where he had been openly speculating as to how many people might be needed to get hold of cattle for the holiday. An informer reported that he had reckoned on 50,000.

Two days before the 12th the Chartist Convention called the Holiday off.The initiative moved to local Chartist groups. In Bradford, Newcastle and most famously in Newport attempts were made to launch an uprising. In November thousands of colliers marched on Newport only to be dispersed by soldiers who killed 24. In Bradford in January 1840 40 Chartists descended on the Green Market, only to find that their plans had been betrayed by an informer. With themselves arrested and Bradford placed under martial law the hoped-for Northern Rising failed to materialise. In the mass arrests that followed local agitators for the Chartists were neutralised country-wide. The Holiday had been postponed. However, although there were no more Chartist initiated strike movements, the idea of the general strike lived on amongst the working class. In 1842 the North was once more racked with strikes. Known as 'The Plug Plot' for the habit of strikers of removing plugs from boilers to cut power off to the factories, it was an independent movement which the Chartist leadership only belatedly supported, attaching their programme to strikes which had already begun for social and economic reasons. Benbow's Northern speaking tours had not been fruitless labour.

Interestingly enough, the subversive life of the Jubilee outlasted that of the Holiday. In a little known incident in Kent in 1838 it inspired agricultural workers to revolt:

> *He told us that all the country would be up, for the great jubilee was to come, and we must go with 'em.*

Led by the bogus knight 'King of the Gypsies', 'King of Jerusalem' Sir William Courtenay, in fact John Tom (son of a Cornish innkeeper) 36 agricultural labourers and small-holders attempted to initiate the millennium. Tom, a scallywag who had been in and out of prison and lunatic asylum, had been in London around 1832 when Benbow's pamphlet made its first impact. Tom took up preaching millennial gospel for some time in the area of North Kent and combined his eschatological ranting with condemnations of the New Poor Law. At the end of May he was leading a small band of his supporters when it met the 45th Infantry Regiment, who had been alerted by the local gentry following Tom's killing of the local constable. In the battle that followed 9 rioters met their deaths, including Tom himself.

The Battle of Bosenden Wood has been called the Last Rising of the Agricultural Labourers[10]. As many people died as at Peterloo, but perhaps its very millenarian character, the fact that it does not fit into radical nostrums of the advance of reason and progress have made it fade from history to become just an episode in a Victorian melodrama.

Jubilee became an aspiration of American Blacks throughout the New World, perhaps brought there by Benbow's revolutionary associate Thomas Wedderburn, son of a slave, and Spencean, perhaps *they* inspired him. Throughout the 19th century the popular songs of Blacks in America resounded with hopes of a Jubilee:

> *De massa run? ha,ha!*
> *De darkey stay? ho,ho!*
> *It mus' be now de kingdom comin'*
> *An' de year ob Jubilo!*
> "Kingdom Coming" **Christy Minstrels** (Composer Henry Clay Work) 1862[11]

And even in England, when the Stockton and Darlington Railway was celebrating its 'Jubilee' in 1875 there were those who had a different version of the idea:

> *At the time of the Railway Jubilee I was a scholar in an adult Sunday School, teached by a few friends intimately connected with the railway. Our lesson for the Sunday morning before the Jubilee was taken from the 25th chapter of Leviticus, which gave me the true meaning of word Jubilee.*

John Wilkinson, leader of 1867 North-East locomotive engineers' strike.[12]

The idea of the grand national holiday faded during the rest of the 19th century. Respectability, moderate reform, modest prosperity, and imperial glory combined to prevent discontent generalising into a grand national movement. The idea of the General Strike was developed on the continent by French and Belgian trades unionists, and was resuscitated in Britain by the rise of syndicalism at the beginning of the 20th century. Arguments about the idea of the General Strike continued within the International Workers movement, with Engels citing the 1839 debacle as a stick with which to beat the Spanish Bakuninists in 1873[13] and Rosa Luxemburg attempting to rescue the idea of the Mass strike in the light of the 1905 Russian Revolution[14]. Perhaps George Sorel came closest to resurrecting the millenarian character of the Grand Holiday with his description of the proletarian general strike as '*a catastrophe, the development of which baffles description*'[15]. The debates reflected the divisions of the day : questions about participation in politics, questions about leadership, none seemed to have been aware of Benbow's pamphlet. Lost amongst all the revolutionary Realpolitik was the idea of the *holiday*, a playful, joyous occasion of conviviality and pleasure. Benbow was certainly as serious a radical as the above luminaries but he didn't lose sight of the origin of revolt, in the longing for ease, gaiety and pleasure. In the century that followed many had cause to regret the absence of such qualities from revolutionary practice.

It might not be too fanciful to suppose that the old strike idea might gain in popularity if we reverted to the old description. Although it is only history now, it is disturbing to be reminded that prior to the Reformation the English enjoyed 150 holidays a year[16] (not including Sundays) and that these festivals involved the total community ceasing from their everyday labours. In other words communal life was radically altered for a third of the year, during which time friendships could be renewed, disputes settled, oppressors challenged, and authority relations reversed. Benbow resurrected the *social* nature of the holiday, albeit for political purposes. It took the development of capitalism, with its relentless imposition of work upon human beings, to make the idea of the holiday a revolutionary idea. In an age of packaged holidays, 'annual leave' and uninterrupted production and consumption, when even time appears as a scarce resource, would not a return to the Holiday that stopped everything rekindle our imaginations as to what life could be?

Notes.

1. W.H. Crook, **The General Strike, Labour's tragic weapon** (1931).
2. Thomas Spence (1750-1814). Advocate of returning land to the people. Major influence on working class radicalism of the time. Considered property relations as important a source of oppression as unrepresentative government.
3. When King George IV accused his wife of infidelity in a bid to remove her from Court she became a populist *cause celebre* which radicals like Benbow used to pillory the monarchy and its hangers-on. (1806-1821).
4. *For it is the ju-bi-le; it shall be holy unto you: ye shall eat the increase thereof out of the field.*
   In the year of this ju-bi-le ye shall return every man unto his possession.
   And if thou sell ought unto thy neighbour, or buyest ought of thy neighbour's hand, ye shall not oppress one another...
   Leviticus 25
5. For information on Spence see Malcolm Chase, **The People's Farm** or P.M.Ashraf, **The Life and Times of Thomas Spence**.
6. For a history of the idea of the Jubilee see Chase 'The Concept of the Jubilee in late 18th and 19th century England' **Past & Present No.129**.
7. See Peter Linebaugh 'Jubilating...' in **The New Enclosures, Midnight Notes**.
8. See Gareth Steadman Jones, **Languages of Class**.
9. Interestingly enough it was the 'conservative' critics of the time, such as Cobbett and Richard Oastler who were more alert to the fact that they were dealing with a system which was radically *new*.
10. See Barry Reay, **The Last Rising of the Agricultural Labourers**.
11. For the story of Jubilee in the Americas see Linebaugh as above.
12. See 'The Concept of the Jubilee...'Chase,as above.
13. F.Engels ,**The Bakuninists at Work** (1873).
13. R. Luxemburg, **The Mass strike, the Political Party, and the Trade Unions** (1906).
15. G.Sorel, **Reflections on Violence** (1908).
16. Witold Rybczinski, **Waiting for the Weekend**.

DEDICATION

TO THE

PRODUCTIVE CLASSES.

PLUNDERED FELLOW-SUFFERERS!

I lay before you a plan of freedom. adopt it, and you rid the world of inequality, misery, and crime. A martyr in your cause, I am become the prophet of your salvation.

A plan of happiness is pointed out and dedicated to you. With it I devote to you my life and body, my soul and blood.

WILLIAM BENBOW.

Commercial Coffee House,
205, Fleet-street.

INTRODUCTORY ADDRESS.

Her princes in the midst thereof are like wolves ravening the prey, to shed blood, and to destroy souls, to get dishonest gain.
The possessors of the land have used oppression, and exercised robbery and have vexed the poor and needy.
EZEKIEL.

LIFE, when good for any thing, consists of ease, gaiety, pleasure, and consequently of happiness. All men enjoy life but do not enjoy it equally. The enjoyment of some is so very limited, that it does not deserve the name of enjoyment; that of others is without bounds, for they have the means of procuring fully ease, gaiety, and pleasure. Thus happiness is circumscribed, and is becoming every day more and more so, that is, the numbers who are deprived of it are hourly increasing. Now, who are they who do enjoy; does their enjoyment proceed from their own merits; are they laborious, — do they work for the happiness they possess ? We shall see. Let nothing but truth, glaring stark-naked truth, be stated.

The only class of persons in society, as it is now constituted, who enjoy any considerable portion of ease, pleasure, and happiness, are those who do the least towards producing any thing good or necessary for the community at large. They are few in number, a fraction, as it were, of society, and yet they have become possessed of a most monstrous power, namely, the power of turning to their own advantage all the good things of life, without creating themselves the smallest particle of any one of those good things. How, in the name of wonder, have they obtained this monstrous power! It must have been either by an involuntary and unnatural consent, or by what seems nearest to the truth by the most stupid ignorance on the part of the people. Of course this monstrous power held by the few is exercised with an iron hand, and necessarily begets indescribable wretchedness and misery among the great mass of society in every part of the kingdom. And this *fraction* of society, to which has been foolishly conceded, or which has impudently and unnaturally usurped, the preposterous right to exercise a monstrous power over almost every man, is as *one* to *five hundred* when compared to the people who produce all the good things seen in the world. Notwithstanding the *one*, the *unit*, the mere *cypher*, has all the wealth, all the power in the state, and consequently prescribes the way and details the manner, after which he pleases the 499 should live in the world. The 499 who create the state, who are its instruments upon all occasions, without whom it cannot go on for a single second, who dig deep, rise early, and watch late, by whose sweat and toil the whole face of nature is beautified — rendered pleasant to the sight, and useful to existence; — the

499 who do all this are reduced to less than nothing in the estimation of the *unit* who does no one thing, unless *consuming* may be called doing something. The one — the unit or cypher — consumes, luxuriates, revels, wastes: in the winter fur and down warm him: in the summer he cools himself in the marble bath or in the shady bower: the seasons are *his* — their flowers, fruits, and living creatures are *his* — the 499 are *his* purveyors, they procure him every thing; and more to be pitied and worse treated than the jackall, they are not left even the offals. Not content with every thing — marrow and bone — if the bone be of any use: not content with their own peculiar titles, this consuming portion of society call themselves the *people!*

They are the *people of substance*, the people of *character*, the people of *condition*, the people of *honor!* so *they* say; but perhaps another definition of what they are would make them more easily recognised. They are the *jugglers* of society, the *pick-pockets*, the *plunderers*, the pitiless *Burkers* — in fine they are all *Bishops!* They exist on disease and blood: crime and infamy are the breath of their nostrils. The 499 bleed for them, die of disease for them; by hard and cruel treatment they are hurried into crime and infamy, if crime and infamy can justly by imputed to beings who make an occasional effort to obtain a portion of the heaps they produce.

The people are formed out of our proportion of 499: they are in number as 499 is to 1. By saying what the people *do*, we explain what they *are*. By saying what they *can* and *ought* to *do*, we explain what they *can* and *ought* to *be*.

For many years the people have done nothing for themselves. They have not even existed, for they have not enjoyed life. Their existence has been enjoyed by others; they have been, as far as regards themselves, *non-entities*. They have had neither ease, gaiety, nor pleasure; they have not lived; for a state of continual toil, privation, and sickness can never be called life. What working man can say he lives ? Unless he says he lives when he is pining away piecemeal, producing with an empty stomach and weary limbs what goes to make others live. The existence of the working man is a *negative*. He is alive to production, misery, and slavery — dead to enjoyment and happiness. He produces and is miserable: others enjoy and are happy. The people then, since we call the mass the people, are the drudges of society; they do every thing and enjoy nothing. The people are nothing for themselves, and every thing for the few.

If they are the source of all wealth — that wealth is not for them: if they are all-powerful, their power is used for the benefit of others: — they protect and support those who grow fat on the sweat of their brow! They fight too; yea, they *fight* — but for what ? for religion, for honour, for the caprice of kings and ministers!

When they fight for *themselves*, then will they be a people, then will they live, then willl they have ease, gaiety, pleasure and happiness; but never, until they do fight for *themselves!* When the people fight their own battle — when they are active in resistance to the greater part of existing institutions — when they have a proper opinion of themselves; that is, when they are convinced of their own power and worth, they will then enjoy the advantages a people ought to enjoy. They will be everything they were not before: they will be no longer abused, maltreated, and lessened in their own estimation: They will be no longer robbed of the fruits of their toil: no longer oppressed and goaded to despair, their lives will be no longer a burden too heavy to be borne. The few — the grasping, the blood-sucking few — will be no longer able to do all this. The few — the idle, dronish few — will be forced to work as well as others, and every man's share of the good things of life will be in proportion to his production of them. When the people are resolved and prepared upon all points to fight their own battle, the rapacity of the landlord, the inhumanity of the king's tax gatherer and of the bishop's tithe proctor will disappear. And if there should happen to be any poor and infirm persons to be provided for, they will not be entrusted to hospital-governors and poor-house keepers, who live in splendour on the parish allowances or charitable donations made solely for the exclusive advantage of the poor and infirm, who may justly be considered, and ought to be treated as the *martyrs of labour !*

How is it that the people have never existed — that is, have not enjoyed ease, gaiety, pleasure, or happiness ? How is it that they have been the instruments of the few, procuring them a superabundance of ease, gaiety, pleasure, and happiness ? How is it that they have always been the *productive* party, and never the *consuming* party ? The lion makes the jackall hunt and provide for him, because the lion is stronger; but, in the case of the people, the position is reversed, for the weaker party have hitherto forced the stronger party to hunt and provide for them. How has this most monstrous state of things been established and kept up ? Simply thus: by keeping the people in ignorance — by hoodwinking them with the bonds of superstition and prejudice.

Ignorance is the source of all the misery of the many. On account of their ignorance they have been oppressed, — plundered, — ground down to the earth, and degraded like beasts of burden. It is ignorance that makes us incessantly toil, not for ourselves, but for others: it is ignorance that makes us fight, and lavish our blood and lives to secure to the few the power of still keeping us their tools; it is ignorance that prevents us from knowing ourselves;

and without a clear knowledge of ourselves we must ever remain the tools of others — the slaves of the consuming party. In every age of the world the people, for want of knowledge of their own worth and power have been the unpaid, unrecompensed tools of kings, nobles, and priests. Yet at no time, in no country, among no people has there existed so much degradation, oppression, and misery, as exists at this moment in this wretched country. Ignorance has reduced England to distraction, and unfortunate Ireland to phrenzied madness.

There is no greater folly than to expect that people will do that which they are ignorant of. To fulfil a duty or to obey a law, we must understand it. Our lawgivers have kept us in ignorance, for if we had knowledge we would not obey laws framed for our own destruction. Our lords and masters are doing every thing that our ignorance may continue, in order that they may continue, like the lawyers of old, "to load us with burdens too grievous to be borne, which they will not touch with one of their fingers." Since our lords and masters have very good reasons for keeping us in ignorance, we have still stronger ones for getting knowledge. By keeping us in ignorance they enjoy: by getting ourselves knowledge we shall enjoy, and *cease* to suffer. The knowledge we want is very easily acquired: it is not that taught in schools or books, or at least in very few books. The knowledge we want is a knowledge of ourselves: a knowledge of our own power, of our immense might, and of the right we have to employ in action that immense power. We cannot have this knowledge without having an opposite kind of knowledge: — namely, the knowledge of the numerical and real weakness of our enemies, though they have been so long enabled to oppress us and drain us to the last drop of our heart's blood. The people of Paris had this knowledge when they revolted against tyranny, and trampled it for a moment under their feet: the people of Paris will give a still stronger example of the sort of knowledge we want, when they declare that kingship and privilege are incompatible with popular liberty: in fine, when they shall strike for a republic — and this example may be expected shortly. The men of Grenoble the other day gave a proof of this knowledge when they refused to pay unjust taxes, burned the tax-gatherers' houses and books, and forced the government to come to a compromise. In short, the knowledge we want is to be fully convinced of the weakness and villainy of our enemies, and to be resolved to use the means we have of destroying them.

The interest of the people has been the same in every age of the world; and yet, extraordinary as it may appear, they have never understood it. If the people had understood their true interests, could any power or accident reduce them to the state they are now in? What that state is we all, alas, know: it is, beyond all contradiction, a state of privation, bordering on starvation, — a state of misery and degradation. Inattention, and the most culpable and dishonourable indifference on their part, have produced their own ruin, and consequently that of the countries they inhabit. Look to the people of this kingdom — look to this country: are they far off from ruin? If you, O people, do not rouse yourselves, you will leave to posterity a nation of the most miserable slaves.

The remedy? the remedy? you all exclaim. You have it within your own reach; but since it seems you cannot see it, you shall have it named to you, and pointed out to you so palpably, that if you do not make use of it, the brand and curse of slavery will stick to you during your wretched lives, and your children and children's children will curse you as traitors, who have sold yourselves, and them, whom you had no right to sell. Now the remedy that is to better your condition, and to snatch you from final and everlasting ruin, is placed within yourselves. It is simply — UNITY OF THOUGHT AND ACTION. — Think together, act together, and you will remove mountains — mountains of injustice, oppression, misery and want. How do you suppose you were brought to your present condition? By never thinking or acting — by being ignorant of yourselves. The bulls in the fable, whilst united, defied the strength of the lion; he sowed jealousy and disunion among them, and they became his prey. Our enemies, by their unity of thought and action — numerically and physically weak as they are — have succeeded in making us their prey. A small portion of mankind, by adopting plan and method, by putting their heads together, have been able to do as they pleased with the greater portion. The smaller portion, by their unanimity, have made the greater portion toil for them: by unity of thought and action, the smaller party have become lords and masters, the greater party slaves.

Lords and masters! They are united; and therefore they may be whatever else they please; they have become, by their unity, lords and masters; and they are, without impunity, the possessors of all power, pomp, greatness, wealth, vanity, lewdness, beastiality, cruelty: — they are a living catalogue of all the vices and crimes that human nature has been forced to be the source of. A want of unity of thought and action on our parts has been the cause of this unnatural state of things. Our indifference and disunion have enabled our horrid enemies to cover the earth with thousands of Sodoms and Gomorrahs.

Of all the follies human nature can be guilty of, there is no one greater than to expect that others will do for us what we ought to do for ourselves. If others do not feel as we do — if they have no cause to feel as we do — if they are not oppressed, robbed, plundered, degraded — how can they enter into our feelings who are so! To expect aid from Tories, Whigs, Liberals — to expect aid from the middling classes, or from any other class than those who suffer, (from the working classes), is sheer madness!

Are liberty and equal rights worth enjoying: are ease, gaiety, pleasure, and happiness worth possessing? Is the satisfaction of seeing ourselves on the same footing with all men — of beholding no longer such a distinction as that between peer and peasant — of no longer seeing ourselves trampled on by the horses and carriages of persons of a different order — of seeing every man either on horseback or on foot, — is such satisfaction worth nothing? What more glorious, more consolatory, more honourable to man than equality! Equality, O people and friends, is grand and beautiful: we may have it; but let us be united!

Virtue — where is it to be found? Among the people! Who have died — who have been martyrs for their principles — the people! Who have been hanged, who have suffered at the stake for their country, and for the good of humanity — the people! From Wat Tyler down to Emmet and Thistlewood, the martyrs of truth have always been found among the people. Their martyrdom would not have been in vain, had we supported them: they relied upon us — they gave us an example — they held forth a torch-light — they sounded a tocsin — their heartstrings wrung it; but we, O shame, have been deaf to it! We have had hearts of steel — we have been worse than the deaf adder; for we have heard the music of liberty, and have not listened to it!

It is almost superfluous to say, that the horrid and merciless tyrants, whom we have allowed to lord it over us, have no feeling in common with us. The whole study of their lives is to keep us in a state of ignorance, that we may not be sensible of our own degradation and of their weakness. To expect good at their hands, to hope that they will break one link of the chain with which they bind us, to dream that they will ever look with pity upon us, is the vainest of all dreams. But enough; they have fattened upon the sweat of our body; they are determined to continue to do so; it is our business to prevent it, to put a stop to it. We are the people, our business is with the people, and to transact it properly, we must take it into our own hands. The people are called upon to work for themselves! We lay down the plan of operation; we despair of all safety, we despair of liberty, we despair of equality, we despair of seeing ease, gaiety, pleasure, and happiness becoming the possessions of the people, unless they co-operate with us. We chalk down to them a plan; woe to them if they do not follow in its traces!

THE HOLIDAY.

A holiday signifies a *holy* day, and ours is to be of holy days the most holy. It is to be most holy, most sacred, for it is to be consecrated to promote — to create rather — the happiness and liberty of mankind. Our holy day is established to establish plenty, to abolish want, to render all men equal! In our holy day we shall legislate for all mankind; the constitution drawn up during our holiday, shall place every human being on the same footing. Equal rights, equal liberties, equal enjoyments, equal toil, equal respect, equal share of production: this is the object of our holy day — of our sacred day — of our festival!

When a grand national holiday, festival, or feast is proposed, let none of our readers imagine that the proposal is new. It was an established custom among the Hebrews, the most ancient of people, to have holidays or festivals, not only religious feasts, but *political* ones. Their feasts were generally held to perpetuate the memory of God's mighty works; to allow the people frequent seasons for instruction in the laws, — to grant them time of rest, pleasure, and renovation of acquaintance with their brethren. The *Sabbath* was a weekly festival, not because they supposed that God reposed from his labour on that day, — but immemorial of their deliverance from Egypt, — out of the house of bondage, and of their feeding on manna in the wilderness. The true meaning of feeding on manna is, that the productions of the soil were equally divided among the people. They fed upon manna — that is they were fed in abundance. During the various festivals, no servile work was done, and servants and masters knew no distinction. Every seventh year, which was called the year of Release, a continued festival was held among the Hebrews. Mark, a holiday for a whole year! How happy a people must be, how rich in provisions, to be able to cease from manual labour, and to cultivate their minds during the space of a whole year! We English must be in a pretty state, if in the midst of civilization and abundance, we cannot enjoy a month's holiday, and cease from labour during the short space of four weeks! But to return, — the year of *release* was a continued — unceasing festival; it was a season of instruction; it was a relief to poor debtors. The land lay untilled; the spontaneous produce was the property of the poor, the fatherless, and the widow; every debt was forgiven, and every bond-servant dismissed free, if he pleased, loaded with a variety of presents from his master. There was another holiday or feast deserving of mention; — it was called the *jubilee*. No servile work was done on it: the land lay untilled; what grew of itself belonged to the poor and needy; whatever debts the Hebrews owed to one another, were wholly remitted; hired, as well as bond servants, obtained their liberty; the holding of lands was changed, so that as the *jubilee* approached, the Hebrew lands bore the less price. By this means landed possession was not confined to particular families, and the sinful hastening to be rich was discouraged.

We have now shewn that the holding of festivals is consecrated by divine authority; it only remains for us to show the necessity that there is for the people of this country holding one; and then to proceed to its details and object.

The grounds and necessity of our having a month's Holiday, arise from the circumstances in which we are placed. We are oppressed, in the fullest sense of the word; we have been deprived of every thing; we have no property, no wealth, and our labour is of no use to us, since what it produces goes into the hands of others. We have tried every thing but our own efforts; we have told our governors, over and over again, of our wants and misery; we thought them good and wise, and generous; we have for ages trusted to their promises, and we find ourselves, at this present day, after so many centuries of forbearance, instead of having our condition bettered, convinced that our total ruin is at hand. Our Lords and Masters have proposed no plan that we can adopt; they contradict themselves, even upon what they name the source of our misery. One says one thing, another says another thing. One scoundrel, one sacrilegious blasphemous scoundrel, says "that over-production is the cause of our wretchedness." Over-production, indeed! when we half-starving producers cannot, with all our toil, obtain any thing like a sufficiency of produce. It is the first time, that in any age or country, save our own, *abundance* was adduced as a cause of *want*. Good God! where is this abundance ? Abundance of food! ask the labourer and mechanic where they find it. Their emaciated frame is the best answer. Abundance of clothing! the nakedness, the shivering, the asthmas, the colds, and rheumatisms of the people, are proofs of the abundance of clothing! Our Lords and Masters tell us, we produce too much; very well then, we shall cease from producing for one month, and thus put into practice the theory of our Lords and Masters.

Over-population, our Lords and Masters say, is another cause of our misery. They mean by this, that the resources of the country are inadequate to its population. We must prove the contrary, and during a holiday take a census of the people, and a measurement of the land, and see upon calculation, whether it be not an unequal distribution, and a bad management of the land, that make our Lords and Masters say, that there are too many of us. Here are two strong grounds for our Holiday; for a CONGRESS of the working classes.

The greatest Captain of the age has acknowledged, that there was partial distress; Londonderry has said, that 'ignorant impatience' was the cause of our misery; the sapient Robert Peel has asserted, that 'our wants proceeded from our not knowing what we wanted.' Very good; during our festival, we shall endeavour to put an end to partial distress; to get rid of our ignorant impatience, and to learn what it is we do want. And these are three other motives for holding a Congress of the working classes.

When Governments disagree; when they have a national right or interest to settle; a boundary to establish; to put an end to a war, or to prevent it; or when they combine to enslave, in order to be able to plunder the whole world, they hold a Congress. They send their wise men, their cunning men, to discuss, plan, and concoct what they call a treaty, and so, at least for a time, settle their differences. In this mode of proceeding there is something that we must imitate. In our National Holiday, which is to be held during one calendar month, throughout the United Kingdom of Great Britain and Ireland, we must all unite in discovering the source of our misery, and the best way of destroying it. Afterwards we must choose, appoint, and send to the place of Congress, a certain number of wise and cunning men, whom we shall have made fully acquainted with our circumstances; and they, before the Holiday be expired, shall discuss and concert a plan, whereby, if it is possible, the privation, wretchedness and slavery, of the great mass of us, may be diminished, if not completely annihilated.

We *affirm* that the state of society in this country is such, that as long as it continues, heart-rending inequality must continue, producing wretchedness, crime, and slavery; — plunging not a few, but the immense majority of the people into those abject circumstances. Our respect and love towards the human race in general, and more especially towards the working classes to whom we belong body and soul, has induced us to reflect and consider, and thus to discover what we think will bring about the object we aim at; namely, the happiness of the many. Our lords and masters, by their unity of thought and action, by their consultations, deliberations, discussions, holidays, and congresses, have up to this time succeeded in bringing about the happiness of the *few*. Can this be denied? We shall then by our consultations, deliberations, discussions, holidays, and congresses, endeavour to establish the happiness of the *immense majority* of the human race, of that far *largest portion* called the *working classes*. What the few have done for themselves cannot the many do for themselves ? unquestionably. Behold, O people and fellow labourers the way!

Before a month's holiday can take place, universal preparations must be made for it. It should not take place neither in seed-time nor in harvest-time. Every man must prepare for it, and assist his neighbour in preparing for it. The preparations must begin long before the time which shall be hereafter appointed, in order that every one may be ready, and that the festival be not partial but universal.

Committees of management of the working classes must be forthwith formed in every city, town, village, and parish throughout the united kingdom. These committees must make themselves fully acquainted with the plan, and be determined to use the extremest activity and perseverance to put into execution as speedily and effectually as possible. They must call frequent meetings, and shew the necessity and object of the holiday. They must use every effort to prevent intemperance of every sort, and recommend the strictest sobriety and economy. The working classes cannot lay in provisions for a month; this is not wanted, but every man must do his best to be provided with food for the first week of the holiday. Provisions for the remaining three weeks can be easily procured. As for wearing apparel, since the holiday will take place in the summer, there can be no great difficulty in being provided with sufficient covering for one month. If the committees do their duty, and earnestly explain the nature and necessity of the holiday, they will induce all lovers of equal rights, to make every sacrifice of momentary inconvenience in order to obtain permanent convenience and comfort.

We suppose that the people are able to provide provisions and funds for one week; during this week they will be enabled to enquire into the funds of their respective cities, towns, villages and parishes, and to adopt means of having those funds, originally destined for their benefit, now applied to that purpose. The committee of management shall be required to direct the people in adopting the best measures that shall be deemed necessary. The people must be made aware of their own folly, in having allowed themselves to have been decived by the Parish parsons, and Select Vestries, and they must cease permitting others to vote away their own money. The people, so soon as they shall see themselves in want of provisions or funds, must have immediate recourse to vestry meetings, which have power to grant, in despite of Overseers and Justices, such relief as maybe wanted. There is nothing to prevent any six or ten persons from calling a vestry meeting as often as may be deemed requisite, and the registers, books, and other parish documents must be consulted, and will give sufficient evidence, that there is wherewithal to support the people during the holiday. Let is be constantly borne in mind, that the united voice of the people will be duly attended to, and that an equal division of funds and provisions will be allowed them by the parish authorities, when their object is known. The committee, which may also be looked upon as the commissary department, must likewise watch over the good order of its district, establish regularity, and punish all attempts at disorder. The people having a grand object in view, the slightest points in their character must be grand. About to renovate Europe, the people must appear renovated.

In the earlier periods of our history, monarchs, princes, and rulers of minor titles, had recourse to voluntary loans. At first the people raised these loans voluntarily, for they thought by so doing, they would enable their chiefs to protect them. It was soon seen, however, that the voluntary loans were converted to the sole advantage of the chiefs, and their more immediate partisans, consequently the people began to grow slack in contributing them. By means of the voluntary loans, the chiefs or governors became powerful enough to exact involuntary loans, and the method of raising them was taxation, and other sorts of exaction. Hence, though sovereignty was at first supported by voluntary loans, as soon as it was discovered to be a self-interested institution, it was obliged to levy involuntary loans, that is, taxes. Now there is a species of sovereignty — we mean the sovereignty of the people — that has not as yet been supported, and it is for its support that we claim at this moment, during the festival that is to establish it, voluntary loans. When we talk of establishing the sovereignty of the people, we talk of establishing the grandeur, the happiness and liberty of the people. Nothing can be more deserving of praise and support. We have hitherto contributed to the sovereignty of particular families, that is to their grandeur, happiness and liberty; and their liberty must be called uncontrolled licence — tyranny.

Now, since we have so long tried the sovereignty of particular families, let us try the sovereignty of the grand family — the human race. That species of sovereignty can never become tyranny. We call then upon every man to add his mite to this voluntary loan, and particularly the rich, who are always so generous in keeping up the splendour of ancient race. The antiquity of the human race they will not allow to be sullied by modern degradation. If they show pity and support towards the descendants of a Stuart, a Bourbon, or a Guelf, they will surely show more towards the descendants of Adam.

"The cattle upon a thousand hills are the Lord's." When the people's voice, which Lord Brougham proclaims to be the voice of God, and surely we need no higher legal authority, calls for its own, demands the cattle of the thousand hills, who dares withold the cattle of the thousand hills ? During our holiday the people may have need of this cattle: let them order it to the slaughter-house, and their herdsmen and drovers will obey them. There may be some persons, who having been so long a time the keepers of the Lord's cattle, will be inclined to keep it still longer. However, we are of opinion, that when solicited they will render "unto the Lord that which is the Lord's." But there are other keepers of the people's cattle, whose unbounded liberality and strict probity are known to the whole world. These keepers may be classed under the denominations of Dukes, Marquesses, Earls, Lords, Barons, Baronets, Esquires, Justices, and Parsons, and they will all freely contribute to our glorious holiday. Some of them, according to the extent of the Lord's flocks, will send us a hundred sheep, others twenty oxen; loads of corn, vegetables and fruit will be sent to each committee appointed by the Lord's voice, which, when distributed among the people, will enable them during the CONGRESS to legislate at their ease, without any fear of want tormenting any part of them.

Should there, however, be a few who may refuse to render up the Lord's cattle, the number of the greatly generous will infinitly counter-balance them. To the NEWCASTLES, who think every thing their own, we will oppose the BURDETTS, who think all they possess, the Lord's or people's. What a faithful keeper of the Lord's cattle we shall find in Sir FRANCIS! The relief we shall obtain from him, when we wait upon him at Belper, Burton, and in Leicestershire, will be a proof of his generosity and probity. The following is the way Sir FRANCIS and all such honest keepers are to be waited on, and our wants and wishes made known to them. Although we name Sir FRANCIS, we do not give him any real preference over the Westminsters, the Russells, the Lansdownes, the Althorpes, &c. Let him, however, be supposed the keeper, that for form sake we are to wait upon. The Committee will depute 20 persons to wait upon Sir FRANCIS, and state to him respectfully, but energetically, their business. Suppose, but it is the most improbable of all suppositions, that Sir FRANCIS should not be inclined to pay full attention to the application. Then the Committee will send 100 persons, with the same request, urging it still more respectfully and energetically; and should there still be indifference on the part of Sir FRANCIS, the Committee shall send 1000 persons, and so on, increasing in proportion, until the Lord's cattle be forthcoming. The persons sent by the Committee, shall allow no one to disturb the peace of the people. Upon all visits from the Committee, the person visited must be seen in person by the Committee: not being at home is no excuse. Sir FRANCIS may be at Belper, Burton, or in Leicestershire; the Committee of those districts will find him at one or either of them, and solicit 'England's glory' for support, which he will freely grant, as he is very rich, and very willing to establish the sovereignty, happiness, and liberty of the people.

Here be it observed, that the above mode of proceeding is not limited to any part of the country, or to any one Sir FRANCIS. All the Sir FRANCISES, all the great reformers are to be applied to, and the people will have no longer any reason to suspect reformers' consistency. The reformers of the united kingdom will hold out an open hand to support us during our festival. O'Connell will abandon the collection made for him; indeed that collection is virtually destined for our Irish brethren during the holiday. Until they are tried no one can imagine the number of great men ready to promote equal rights, equal justice, and equal laws all throughout the kingdom.

When all the details of the above plan are put into execution, the committee of each parish and district, shall select its wise men to be sent to the NATIONAL CONGRESS. A parish or district having a population of 15,000 four, a population of 25,000 eight, and London fifty wise and cunning men. The advice of the different committees is to be taken as to the most convenient place for conference. It should be a central position, and the mansion of some great liberal lord, with its out houses and appurtenances. The only difficulty of choice will be to fix upon a central one, for they are all sufficiently vast to afford lodging to the members of the Congress, their lands will afford nourishment, and their parks a beautiful place for meeting.

It may be relied upon, that the possessor of the mansion honoured by the people's choice, will make those splendid preparations for the representatives of the sovereignty of the people, that are usually made for the reception of a common sovereign.

The object of the Congress; that is what it will have to do. To reform society, for "from the crown of our head to the sole of our foot there is no soundness in us." We must cut out the rottenness in order to become sound. Let us see what is rotten. Every man that does not work is rotten; he must be made work in order to cure his unsoundness. Not only is society rotten; but the land, property, and capital is rotting. There is not only something, but a great deal rotten in the state of England. Every thing, men, property, and money, must be put into a state of circulation. As the blood by stagnation putrifies, as it is impoverished by too much agitation, so society by too much idleness on the one hand, and too much toil on the other has become rotten. Every portion must be made work, and then the work will become so light, that it will not be considered work, but wholesome exercise. Can any thing be more humane than the main object of our glorious holiday, namely, to obtain for all at the least expense to all, the largest sum of happiness for all.

We think that the necessity of a GRAND NATIONAL HOLIDAY has been fully impressed upon the mind of every man who may have read us.

We have etched out the plan; not detailed and matured it, for it will take a longer time and deeper reflection before we can pronounce our plan complete. We expect the assistance of others, and we invite them, without putting us to unnecessary expence, to communicate to us their hints. We have explained in a few words our object: it will be seen that never was there an object, an aim so sublime, so full of humanity. We will not revert, now that we are forced to a conclusion, to the necessity of a holiday, but we must repeat ourselves respecting the plan.

We are sure that there is no one who will not be ready to join heart and hand in our festival, provided he can be persuaded of the possibility of holding it. If we had not been convinced of the possibility of holding it, we should never have mentioned it. All we require is that our holiday folk should be prepared for *one* week; we engage ourselves to provide for all their wants during the last three weeks of the festival. We have shown in what way the people should have recourse to vestry meetings, and what power they had over all parish authorities. We have shown that the parish authorities are entirely dependent on the people, and that without the consent of the people they can raise no rate, nor dispose of any fund already accumulated. We have shewn that the people had a right to examine the parish accounts, and become cognizant of the funds held by the parish authorities, and that the people could dispose of those funds as they thought proper. If, then, there are funds in hand, the people will apply them to their own support during the holiday; if it should happen that there are not funds, the people must vote a supply, for the people must be convinced of one thing, namely, that it is they alone who have a right of levying parish contributions. Some few persons may not like the idea of having recourse to parish allowance for their support even during the short period of three weeks, but these over-delicate individuals must reflect that they are becoming a *momentary* burden to their parish, in order to rid it of increasing, and *everlasting* burdens. We think we have said enough to prove, that by vestry meetings alone the people would be fully able to support themselves during the holiday. Let the people only reflect on the sums that the parish authorities have from time immemorial levied upon the people, without the concurrence of the people, and then they will have no longer any scruples, but will, if the occasion require it, have recourse to the same method for raising funds for the benefit of the many, that the few have always had for the benefit of the few. We are too honest, too conscientious, too delicate, consequently the few who are neither honest, conscientious nor delicate dupe us. We must avoid all squeamishness; we are not only working for ourselves but for the human race and its posterity. We beg of the people to thrown off all false delicacy. They must boldly lay hands upon that which is their own.

We call our reader's attention to what we have said about "the cattle upon the thousand hills." They are the Lord's, that is the people's; and when the people want them, the guardians who have kept them so long, will deliver them unto the people. We repeat, and we do so expressly that the people may be the more convinced of what we assert, that Sir FRANCIS BURDETT, and all such liberal men, will come forward in shoals to support us. There is nothing enthusiastic or ideal in this assertion. Let us reflect upon it. MR. COKE, of Norfolk, is a very rich man, and a very liberal man. Now we ask, what does a liberal man amass wealth for, if not in order to be able to support liberal principles. MR. COKE'S heart will beat with joy when he finds such an occasion for his liberality, as we are going to give him. We see him already ringing for his check-book, and ordering droves of his oxen, and waggon-loads of his wheat to be sent to us holiday folks. We hear him swearing at his servants, damning their laziness, when the demands of the people are to be satisfied. And in every county a COKE is to be found; in Middlesex you will find a BYNG, in Bedfordshire a WHITBREAD. It would be too long to mention names, but you have only to look over the list of the majority in the House of Commons on the Reform Bill, and the list of the minority in the House of Lords on the same Bill, and then you will see, at a glance, the number of liberal men who are keeping their riches for your advantage. Only think of the immense sums that these liberal men spend at elections, in order to legislate for you, and consequently do you good! Now can you be persuaded, that they will not liberally resist you when you are fighting your own battle. Be assured they will; not only will they send you funds and provisions, but you will find them simple volunteers in your ranks. HENRY BROUGHAM, Lord Chancellor, will, if you accept of him, volunteer his services as one of your Deputies to CONGRESS. These great men, O people, are waiting for you; as soon as they can rely upon you, you may rely upon them. All they want to declare themselves for you, is your support. Let them have it.

We intended to give a list of the principal subjects to be discussed and settled during our CONGRESS. The Public shall have this list in a Periodical, advertised on the last page.

FINIS.

Pub. Sept 10 1820 by Benbow's Corner of St Clement's Church

K—G CUPID in the CORNER—Playing Bopeep.

A Selection of Erotica from *The Rambler's Magazine*(1822)

There was no great distinction for Benbow between publishing pornography or publishing polemics against the state. For Benbow erotica was just another commodity that the aristocracy wished to keep for themselves. Making it available to the poor was another way the system of organised scarcity could be subverted:

> *The works that he has published contain no more obscenity than are to be met within every novel that is published, they contain by no means so much lasciviousness as the writings of Shakespear, and scores of other great geniuses whose productions appear continually on the stage, and which have obtained for their authors immortal praise. He need not mention, Rabelais, Sterne or Voltaire, he need not produce a catalogue of all our poets, including the most chaste, and then ask whether he has published any thing immoral, indecent or lascivious. He need not advert to the numerous exhibitions of naked female figures , daily exhibiting to the public, he need not bring to the recollections of his readers, the amatory passages in the word of God, to give them the best name, to prove that love, in an overwhelming majority, has been the principal theme of all the principal authors.Can anything more expose the abominable hypocrisy of these confederated wretches, who thus club their extortions from the labours of the community, to destroy and ruin those who may give them offence....*
> *This state of the press is worse than censorship; as now everything is a libel that these scoundrels chuse to call so. If extracts from esteemed writers be libels, then he will acknowledge himself guilty; but, till he finds that they attack the rich as well as the poor, he shall consider them oppressors, and abominable hypocrites. Works have been published, and that lately too, which are grossly obscene and immoral, but, because they were patronised by the great they were suffered to circulate freely. How long such a state of things must exist is not for him to tell, but while it does, no man can consider himself free... Benbow in Rambler's Magazine 1/12/1822*

The 'confederated wretches' he was talking about were **The Society for the Suppression of Vice,** a body of the great and the good who had taken upon themselves the duty of monitoring the morals of the people. In 1822 they were to take Benbow to court over the publication of *The Rambler's Magazine*(*RM*). They appear to have been particularly incensed by the translation of *Les Amours du Chevalier de Faublas* , extracts of which are reprinted here, and which Benbow and his associate George Cannon[1] published in full in the same year. It is uncertain whether it was the author's Jacobin connections, the fact that the extract included cross-dressing and sexual ambiguity, or that it mocked the aristocracy, which piqued the Society. In court the Lord Chancellor described the *RM* as 'extremely seductive' which may say more about the Lord Chancellor than anything else, and ordered all extant copies to be destroyed. Benbow had to collect up all the traceable copies and hand them over to the court. In all 2,850 were handed in to be burned. One copy still exists in the British Library.

Prior to Cannon and Benbow's efforts libertinist texts tended to be made available to the well-off only - Cleland's *Fanny Hill, Memoirs of a Woman of Pleasure* is perhaps the most famous example of this genre. Cannon justified pornographic publication because sex was a natural pleasure :

> *In yielding to the dictates of love, and of performing its joyful rites, we are subscribing to the religion of NATURE; we are pious without hypocrisy, and our fervour arises from real instead of pretended inspiration. Our devotion is not the discipline of gloomy bigots, but the ardent enthusiasm of zealous votaries, who are prompted by a love of heaven, and not goaded by a fear of hell.'On Love'(RM 1/12/1822)*

The pleasure of erotica made it not only an anti-clerical weapon, but also undermined all ideologies which were based on fear and self-denial.

Given Benbow's support of the rowdy pleasure-seeking side of London radicalism publishing these writings was just a development of an already existing culture of transgression,experiment and putting the body before the spirit. He had already milked to the utmost satisfaction of the underworld and the utmost discomfiture of the ruling party the bawdy tradition of political satire in the Queen Caroline affair (see print reproduced here). At a time when moral order, thrift and respectability began to become positive values for some in the radical movement, publishing erotica and exposing the sexual pecacadillos of the powerful sustained the disreputable trend in radicalism. While luminaries such as Richard Carlile and Francis Place disapproved, this bawdy tradition ensured that radical politics kept circulating amongst those for whom respectability and decorum were neither possible nor desirable.

Benbow's publishing instincts were for the full disclosure of knowledge and culture (before the publication of *RM* he had secretly printed the theories of the surgeon W.Lawrence who questioned the idea of the separation between the soul and the body). In the *RM* this meant the production of a style of puritanism and prurience which, separated from its radical politics, became the house-style of the conformist popular press.

Benbow's publishing work was an implicit attack on the growing tide of middle class paternalism that did so much to undermine the self-confidence necessary for a successful revolt against the British state. This curious mix of control and enlightenment proved more deadly to revolt than all the physical repressions put together. It's a legacy still being dealt with today.

1. George Cannon. Middle class renegade.Spencean and radical pornographer.Ended up as publisher of flagellation texts who eventually died in a House of Correction in 1854.See **Radical Underworld** : Iain McCalman.

Acknowledgements.

Thanks to Pete Smith for nursing my computer during all the drafts and re-drafts of the introductions, to Mike Peters and Malcolm Stroud for critical remarks, to Linda Lee and Jane Gregson for typesetting the original pamphlet, and to Pam Buck and Maureen Clark for collating and stapling the finished product.

Les Amours du Chevalier de Faublas

This elegant and fascinating Romance, was first published in the year 1787. It was written by LOUVET, de Couvray, a member of the Jacobin club, and one of the founders of the French Revolution. We understand that a *mutilated* translation was published, about twenty years since, which is now entirely out of print, and very rarely to be met with. As the original is so universally read and admired, and an English edition being much called for, a new and faithful translation has been made, and will be immediately printed in two neat pocket volumes, without any curtailment. Being confident that it is a work which will suite the taste of all our readers, we are happy in being able to give them a specimen of it, before publication. The part which we shall select, is where young Faublas, when sixteen, is induced by his friend the Count Rosambert, to put on female attire, and go to a ball with him, in order to mortify a mistress of the Count's. The youth and appearance of Faublas, suiting well for this metamorphosis it was presently put in execution, and leave obtained from his father, for him to continue at the ball all night :-

*******"I am going" said the Count to me," to present you to a young lady that I esteem very much; it is full two months since I have sworn an eternal attachment to her, and more than six weeks that I have proved it to her." This language was quite enigmatical to me, but already I began to blush at my ignorance, and I put on a knowing smile, to make Rosambert think that I understood him. "As I am going to torment her," continued he, "assume an air as if you loved me very much, you see what effect it will make on her! Above all, let me caution you against telling her that you are not a girl. We shall be sure to mortify her."

As soon as we appeared in the assembly, all the eyes were fixed on me; I was vexed to feel that I blushed, and could not keep my countenance. Sometimes I thought that a part of my dress must be out of order, or that my borrowed character had betrayed me; but presently, from the general attention of the men, and the universal discontent of the women, I judged that I was well disguised. One lady threw at me a disdainful look; another examined me with a pouting air; they agitated their fans, they whispered among themselves, and smiled maliciously. I saw that I received such a welcome with which they honour, in a numerous circle, a rival who is too pretty, when she appears for the first time.

A very handsome woman entered; it was the mistress of Rosambert. He presented to her his relation, who came, said he from a convent. The lady (who was called the Marchioness B***) welcomed me in the most obliging manner; I took a seat by her, and the young folks formed a semicircle round us. The Count, much pleased to excite the jealousy of his mistress, affected to give me

Mars, Venus, & Vulcan.

Leda.

a marked preference - The Marchioness, apparently piqued at his coquetry, and fully resolved to punish him, in concealing from him her resentment, redoubled her politeness towards me: "Mademoiselle, have you a taste for the convent?" said she to me -"I should like it well, madam, if I found there many persons like yourself." The Marchioness testified by a smile, how much this compliment flattered her; she put several other questions to me, and appeared delighted with my answers. She loaded me with the little caresses which the women lavish on each other; told Rosambert, that he was happy in having such a relation, and finally gave me a tender kiss, which I returned very politely.
This was neither what Rosambert wished, nor what he had promised himself. Hurt at the vivacity of the Marchioness, and still more at the readiness with which I received her caresses, he whispered into her ear, and discovered to her the secret of my disguise." A very likely tale!" cried the Marchioness, after having regarded me for a few moments: the Count protested he had told her the truth. - She looked at me again:"What folly! It cannot be." The Count renewed his protestations. "What an idea!" replied the Marchioness, and dropping her voice:"Do you know what he says? He insists that you are a young man disguised." I answered timidly, in a low voice, that he said the truth. The Marchioness darted a tender look at me, gently squeezed my hand, and pretending to have misunderstood me:" I know it well," said she, sufficiently loud;"it has not the shadow of probability." Then addressing the Count; "But sir, to what end are all these jokes?" "What !" replied he to this, with astonishment, "Does mademoiselle pretend" - "How, if she pretends! look at her! a child so amiable! so pretty!" - "What!" said the Count again - "Oh! sir, do pray drop this nonsense," continued the Marchioness, in a manner peculiarly piquante;" You either take me for a fool, or you are mad yourself."

I began seriously to think she had not understood me; I said in a low tone: "I beg your pardon, madam, I have, perhaps, badly explained myself; I am not what I appear to be; the Count has told you the truth." "I do not believe you, anymore than him," replied she, speaking still lower than myself, and squeezing my hand. -" I assure you madam" - "Hold your tongue, you are an hypocrite; but you shall not deceive me any more than him";and she embraced me. Rosambert, who had not heard us , remained stupefied. The young folks who surrounded us, seemed to wait with as much curiosity as impatience the end and explanation of a dialogue so obscure to them; but the Count, restrained by the fear of offending his mistress if he covered himself with ridicule, and also flattering himself, that I should presently put an end to the mistake; bit his lips, and dared not say a word. Happily at this moment, the Marchioness saw her friend the Countess C*** enter the ball-room: I know not what she whispered into her ear, but the Countess immediately attached herself to Rosambert, nor quitted him during the evening....

The Marchioness had not lost sight of me for an moment; I wished to rest myself, I found a place near her; we began, and re-began, broke off, and began twenty times, a very animated conversation, which was often interrupted by caresses, and in which I saw plainly, that I must leave her in the error which appeared to please her so much.

The Count did not cease to observe us with great inquietude, but the Marchioness would not appear to see him: "My intention,"said she to me,"is not to pass the whole night here, and if you take my advice, you will be careful of your health. Come home and have some slight refreshment with me; it is past midnight. Monsieur, the Marquis, will not be long in coming to join me; we will go and sup, and I will afterwards conduct you to your own house, you will find the Marquis a very singular man. He has occasionally fits of tenderness for me - at other times caprices of jealousy, very ridiculous, and frequently is inclined to pay me attentions with which I could willingly dispense. When he vows fidelity to me, I neither believe it nor care for it; nevertheless I shall not be sorry to put him to the proof: he will see you and find you charming. You will not begin then with this pretty tale of disguise; 'tis an amusing joke, but we have worn it out; therefore, instead of repeating it before the Marquis of B***, you will do well, if you have no objection to oblige me a little, to make him some advances." I demanded of her what advances she meant. She laughed heartily at the simplicity of my question, and then regarding me with a tender look: "Hear me," said she, "it is clear that you are a woman: therefore, all the carresses which I have given you this evening, are only out of friendship: but if you had indeed been a young man disguised, and believing it, I had treated you in the same manner, that would have been called making advances, and very warm ones too." I promised her to make advances to the Marquis. - "Very well; smile at his proposals, look at him in a significant manner, but do not let him press your hand as I have done, nor embrace you as I have embraced you; that would be neither proper nor decent."

The Marquis arrived. He still had a young look: he was well made, but of very small stature; his appearance was gay, but the gaiety was of that sort which always causes a laugh at its expense. "Here is Mademoiselle du Portail," said the Marchioness (for I had taken that name) "she is a young relation of the Count, you will thank me for having introduced her to you, she is kind enough to sup with us." The Marquis found that I had *a very happy physiognomy,*he lavished on me the most ridiculous eulogiums, and I returned them by the most extravagant compliments. "I am very happy, Mademoiselle," said he, in a formal manner, which he thought very fine, "that you do me the honour to sup with me; you are very pretty - very pretty, and you may depend on what I say in that respect, for I am skilled in physiognomy. "My dear child,"said the Marchioness, "you have given me your word, you are to polite to break it; I will disembarrass you of the Marquis as soon as he becomes tiresome": she squeezed my hand, and the Marquis saw it. "Oh! that I might press one of those little hands within mine!" said he. I cast at him a scornful glance: "Let us go, ladies, let us go," cried he with an air of levity and triumph, and went out to call his servants.

Rosambert, who heard him, came to us notwithstanding the efforts of the Countess to restrain him: "Monsieur" (said he to me, in a tone of serious irony) "you no doubt find your new dress very convenient, and do not intend to undeceive the Marchioness." "I replied in the same tone, but lowering my voice: "My dear kinsman, would you so soon destroy your own work?" He addressed himself to the Marchioness: "I feel myself bound in conscience, madam, to warn you once more, that it is not Mademoiselle du Portail who will have the Honour to sup with you, but the Chevalier du Faublas, my very young and very faithful friend." "And I, sir, declare to you, that you have reckoned too much on my credulity and my patience. Have the goodness to drop this impertinent badinage, or determine never to see me more."- "I have the courage to chuse either the one or the other, madam, but I should be sorry to interfere with your pleasures, by my indiscretions, or balk them by my importunities."

The Marquis re-entered at the same moment; he tapped Rosambert on the shoulder, and holding him by the hand, said: "What do you not sup with us? Do you leave your relation with us! Know you that she is pretty! Know you what her physiognomy promises!" He lowered his voice:"But between us, I think the little creature is somewhat - lively." "Oh! yes, very pretty, and very lively," replied the Count, with a sarcastic smile; "She resembles many others";and then, as if he had predicted the approaching fate of this good husband; "I wish you a good night," said he. "What! think you",replied the Marquis, "that I keep your relation for?" - "Listen then, if she is desirous! - I wish you a good night," repeated the Count, and he went out laughing heartily. The Marchioness contended that Rosambert had become mad; and I considered that he was very impolite. "Not at all," said the Marquis, confidently to me, "He loves you to distraction: he has observed that I pay court to you, and he is jealous."

In five minutes we were at the residence of the Marquis. Supper was served up immediately, and I was placed between the Marchioness and her gallant spouse, who never ceased saying to me, what he thought, very pretty things. Too much occupied at first in satisfying an appetite, rather masculine, which dancing had given me, I did not find time to reply to him, except by the language of the eyes. As soon as my hunger was a little abated, I applauded, without exception, all the foolish things that he had been pleased to utter, and his bad *bon mots* produced him a hundred compliments, with which he was enchanted. The Marchioness, who had all along paid me the greatest attention, and whose looks were visibly animated, possessed herself of one of my hands. Curious to see how far the power of my deceitful charms extended, I abandoned the other to the Marquis, who seized it with an inexpressible transport.

The Marchioness, plunged into the most profound reflections, seemed meditating some important project; I observed her blush, and tremble by turns, and without saying a word, she gently pressed my right hand, which she held within her own. But my left hand was in a prison less agreeable; the Marquis squeezed it in a manner that made me cry out. Charmed with his good fortune, proud of his happiness, and astonished at the address with which he deceived his wife, even in her own presence, he began alternately to heave deep sighs, and to burst into fits of laughter, which made the ceiling ring; at length, fearing to betray himself, and wishing to stifle his laughter, which the Marchioness might notice, and also, perhaps, thinking thereby to convince me of his passion he bit my fingers.

The beautiful Marchioness waking from her reverie, said: "Mademoiselle du Portail, it is late; you were to have passed the whole night at the ball, and they do not expect you at home before eight or nine o'clock in the morning; stay, therefore with me. I offer to anyone an apartment in my house, but my own room shall be at your service. I ought," added she, in an affectionate tone, "to act as your mamma; and I would not that my daughter should have any other room to sleep than my own; I will go and make up a little bed for you, near mine".- "And why make up a bed," interrupted the Marquis,"There is quite room enough for two in your own: when I come to you there, shall I incommode you? I sleep all night, and so do you." Having said this, he gave me in an amorous manner, beneath the table, so hard a blow on the knee, that it grazed the skin. I instantly replied to this gallantry in the same manner, and so vigorously, that he uttered a loud cry. The Marchioness rose with an air of alarm. "It is nothing" ,said he, "I have only hit my leg against the table." I burst with laughter, the Marchioness could no more restrain herself than me, and her dear spouse, without knowing why, began to laugh still louder than us both.

When our excessive gaiety was a little moderated, the Marchioness renewed her offers. "Accept the half of the Marchioness' bed," cried the Marquis, "Accept it, I beg of you, you will be well there, you will be very comfortable indeed there. I am going for the present, but do pray, in the meantime accept her offer." He left us. "Madam", said I to the Marchioness, "Your invitation is as flattering as it is agreeable, but, is it for Mme. du Portail, or Monsieur de Faublas that you intend it?" "What ! the Count's bad jokes over again, you little rogue! and do you repeat them! Have I not told you, that I do not believe you?" "But madam "- "Peace, peace," replied she, putting her hand on my mouth; "The Marquis is coming, let him not hear such nonsense as this. What a charming girl!"said she, embracing me tenderly, "How timid and how modest she is! but she is also very

The Agreeable Ghost.

whimsical, come on, you little pickle, come," she held out her hand to me, and we passed into her chamber.

I hesitated about going to bed....A chambermaid passed near me at the very last moment when I was pulling off the last petticoat, I trembled lest she should open the curtains; I jumped into bed, astonished at the singular adventure which brought me there, but not as yet suspecting that in sleeping together, we should have any other desire than of chatting together, before we went to sleep. The Marchioness was not long in following me, we heard the voice of her husband; "These ladies might as well permit me to assist them in going to bed!" He wanted to embrace me; the Marchioness was greatly offended; he closed the curtains himself, and bade us goodnight.

A profound silence reigned for some moments. "Are you asleep already, my sweet child," said the Marchioness in a gentle tone - "Oh! no I am not asleep." She threw herself into my arms, and pressed me against her bosom. "Oh heaven!" cried she, with an astonishment very naturally assumed, "It is a man!" and then quickly repulsing me, "What, is it possible ?" - "Madam," replied I, trembling, "I told you so: ... Pardon me, madam, be not angry; I am going to recline in the armchair." "Yes undoubtedly you must - but what a fine resource (still holding me by the arm) fatigued as you must be! to remain in the cold, and to injure your health! You deserve that I should treat you with this rigour - well, rest there, but promise that you will be prudent." "Provided madam, that you will pardon me" - "No, I do not pardon you! but I have still more regard for you, than you have for me. see how cold your hand is already!" And out of pity she put it on her ivory bosom. Guided by nature, and by love, this happy hand descended a little; I know not the stimulus which caused my blood to boil. "No woman", said the Marchioness in a milder tone, "Ever experienced the embarrassment in which you place me." "Ah! pardon me my dear mamma!" - "Your dear mamma, indeed ! you have a great regard for dear mamma, little libertine that you are!" Her arms which had first repulsed me, gently drew me towards her; presently we were so close to each other, that our lips came in contact, and I was emboldened to print a burning kiss upon hers. "Faublas" , said she, in a voice scarcely audible: "Is this what you promised me?" Her hand strayed; a raging flame circulated in all my veins - "Ah madam! pardon me, I die" - "Ah my dear Faublas - my friend-" I continued motionless. The Marchioness felt for my embarrassment, which did not displease her - She kindly aided my inexperience, and I received with as much astonishment as pleasure, a charming lesson, which I repeated more than once.